Poetic Pieces

By Raymond M. Simmons

Poems herein are the products of Raymond Simmons and he is responsible for these contents. Wider Perspectives Publishing reserves 1st run of printing rights, but all materials reverts to property of the author at time of delivery. All rights to republication thereafter fall to the author and he may submit items to contests and anthologies at will.

Thank you to Delroy Simmons, coauthor of *We're Not Old*

1st run released June 2019 Hampton Roads, Virginia

copyright 2019 Raymond M. Simmons
1st edition ISBN 9781078499231
2nd Edition 2020, **ISBN: 978-1-952773-04-4**

INTRODUCTION

My goal is to enlighten as much as the confines of my modest efforts will allow. I pray that in my own humble way I can inspire others with my efforts, and promote mankind's appreciation for beauty, his capacity for love, his need for humanity, and his dedication to brotherhood. If the words I write can touch one soul, change one mind and promote some bliss, then this book will have served its purpose.

DEDICATION

Once again I dedicate this book to the memory of my dear mother who deserved much more credit than my lack of insight was able to give. Only now that she is no longer of this earth can I sum up the essence of her solid character. Mistakes and miscues came with her humanity, as it does with us all. I find that any mistakes or wrong doing on her part, no way measured up to the soul of goodness that she instilled in my siblings and myself. Thanks for the memories mom. I have no doubt that you have received God's blessings.

THANKS

Thanks to J. Scott Wilson and Tanya Cunningham, who work so hard to allow humble poets like me to spread our words and gain some kernel of recognition as we exonerate the treasure of literary nugget which spills from our minds.
Thanks to Ann Shalaski and the Word for Word poets, who are in many ways responsible for my maturity as a poet. They made me strive to be a better poet. They also made me realize that I can always do better. Thanks to all the other poets who have bonded and formed a warm, tight, supportive and understanding group. You are my brothers and sisters and we will always be family.

Tell me not in mournful number that life is just an empty dream.
(Henry Wadsworth Longfellow)
It's not if you love the dream you're living.

POETIC PIECES

And the Award Goes to…	2
Angels and Magicians and Gods	4
Adam's First Thoughts	6
Playing Ball	8
Love of Games	10
Angry Players	12
Keepers of the Gold	14
You Talk too Much	16
Bragging	18
Ego	20
The Good Guys	22
Texting and Driving	26
What Do We Have to Sing About	28
Young Hustlers	30
Clouded Identity	32
I Remember When	34
Open Mic	36
Damaged Goods	38
Secret Crush	40
Wish I Were Superman	42
Diamond in the Rough	44
Hero Worship	46
Honest Politicians	48
Why Do My Dogs Like You?	50
I Owe Myself an Apology	52
Amazing Me	54

Planet Earth	56
Tribal Skins	58
The Snob	60
Senseless Things	62
Reconnection	64
Real Beauty	66
Ode to My Guitar	68
Someday	70
Success	72
Bittersweet	74
Taking Things for Granted	76
Temptation	78
The Lost Souls of Abortions	80
The Abyss	82
The Boston Tea Party	84
Tribute to the Bus Driver	86
The Enchanted Disconnect	88
Harvey and Irma	90
Writers Block	92
We're Not Old	94
Evolution	96
The Court Room	98
Family Reunion	100
Epiphany	102
Worried Mind	104
Peace of Mind	108
Appendix on Rhyme	110

AND THE AWARD GOES TO...

You should have won the Oscar
For your skill at playing your part.
Your sound performance in each scene
Was well played to break my heart.

You knew what made me laugh and cry.
You made me think we were perfect.
You had a sexy blink and sigh.
You really knew how to worked it.

Your great performance accented
Every dramatic scene you tried.
Your talent well represented,
You took me along for the ride.

I never heard anyone yell
For lights, or camera, or action,
Yet every scene was played so well
And you were the main attraction.

As every scene became your own,
You were director, star, and crew,
Voiding distraction with a groan.
Forcing eyes to focus on you,

Though sometimes numb with weariness,
Faithfully I carried your gear.
I believed it was for the best,
Because it soothed your deepest fear.

You threw up so many defenses,
I didn't see the plot get thicker,
And when I came to my senses,
I had been cut from the picture.

I was a prop to bide your time.
It took a while to understand,
That I was never on your mind,
And never in your future plan.

Things are clear, no longer confused.
My once blind eyes now opened wide.
New angles show me different views,
I have found what you tried to hide.

I was banned from your studio.
There was no begging or pleading.
I chose then to quietly go.
No knee pads would I be needing.

We never got to settle this,
Your movie I never did see.
You yelled wrap and I was dismissed.
That's cool, I hated your movie.

So watch, view and edit it.
That's what you always wanted.
You'll selfishly take all credit,
And be thoroughly self-vaunted.

There's no single doubt in my mind
That your name will grace every line.
From the start this was your project
To the end you are the subject.
And the Oscar goes to….

ANGELS AND MAGICIANS AND GODS

So many things we seem to know,
Focused and void of base desire.
We came to earth on ships of fire,
More rapid than a comets flow.

We should have moved on in space
From this strange potent addiction.
All options have now been erased,
And our future has grim predictions.

We floated here through time and space,
Our logic played a special part.
We navigated to this place,
Where legacies have touched our heart.

And now it seems we've lost our pace,
We feel forsaken and confused.
We should have shunned this horrid place,
Where we have been grossly abused.

For we are brothers to the rocks,
Entrapped inside these human walls.
We all stand helpless to the clock,
Feeling weak and destined to fall.

When we paused at earth's station
Our power lost its magic touch.
It matters not the location
The awe of Earth is just too much.

And now we are just out of luck,
Captured enthralled and complacent.
We are bound abandoned and stuck,
This dwelling is now our essence.

Your breed is strange and hard to please,
Your good will seems lost and unkind.
Your essence swells with mysteries,
And seek the answers hard to find.

And all the lives we tried to save,
Your backward schemes did sacrifice.
Although we took you from your cave,
You still ignored our sound advice.

Clear-cut lessons should have prevail
As you approached maturity,
But instead you found ways to fail,
And worthy souls you'll never be.

All your solutions are right here,
As we guide and watch over you.
We're not supposed to interfere,
So there's not much that we can do.

Since your priority is pride,
On wisdom you are less than strong.
Your words and games will never hide
So many things that you get wrong.

ADAM'S FIRST THOUGHTS (Maybe)

Is this me, who am I? What am I?
What am I, but some complicated human
Contraption of harmonious working parts
That touch all degrees of existence,
And yet leaves me completely baffled?

What is this rare strange substance called flesh,
That fills my body and dwells inside me,
With various thickness, and mystic degrees?
What is this silent noise inside my head,
That speaks a language without a voice?

I am aware of abstract things,
And somehow know everything's name.
I know the presence of the mysterious air.
I am aware of thought and imagination
That shows me things that are not there.

Everything is in accord with my delicate mind.
Cryptic harmony cast gloomy human design.
All of my realities are observed
With this new enchantment I'm served.
New potions fuel and generate this status of life,
That holds my spirit inside, and leaves my tongue tied,
Because it bears no instructions or guides.

Embarking on this glorious mystical ride,
A phenomenon I know is time.
Time is something that my minuscule brain,
And imagination cannot understand or explain.
It accompanies me through its stages,
And takes my existence to phases,
Where my body surrenders its youth.
Some secrets my confused senses cannot smell,
See, feel, hear, comprehend, conquer or taste.

I can only observe that I am set here
On this huge earth stage under its
Enormous precisely timed spotlight.
The concept fills me with Anxiety.

Where does my humble existence and worth
Fit into the grand design and splendor divine?
My newfound self with my delicate imagination,
Can only assume some random meanings,
Due to my lack of understanding of specific meanings.

As I insert myself in this river of time,
I am completely oblivious of my origin,
And as I float to my unknown destination
like dust in the wind adrift in the universe,
I know not what I should search or reach for
Or what I should expect to find
Yet I know that something is missing,
As I sink I am surrounded by the folds of time.

PLAYING BALL

Crying for blood and violence,
Anxious to see the consequence.
Like gory Roman patriarchs,
Impatient for the fight to start.

Their mob-like roars are all around,
I'm on the field, I hear the sound.
They're watching every move I make
To see if I got what it takes.

They shout "hit with velocity",
That's what they all expect to see.
Within me I find thuggish wrath,
As I plow through and make my path.

Ball carrier must not move forth,
I send them south when they head north,
And if I stop them in their track,
My coach will stand and cheer for that

Can't play for fun, that's not enough.
My coaches say I must play rough.
The coaches make headstrong demands,
But my pain they don't understand.

When I attack at such high speed.
Relief from pain is what I'll need.
When I cause pain to someone else.
I also bring it to myself.

The coaches only recognize,
The pride they feel winning the prize.
They say that I must endure pain,
They just exclaim no pain no gain.

And through this entire process,
Their bodies never feel my stress.
They stand back and manipulate
In complete control of my fate.

I'm the one who take all the hits,
On practice fields with dirt filled pits.
We practice in the rain and mud,
Tasting dirt and ignoring blood.

Filling my head with false desires,
The coaches scheme to light my fire.
To convince me that my only claim
Is my love for this violent game.

Steady fed by blind ambition.
They speak of owed recognition,
And in reality, their only concerns,
Are winning records they will earn.

What the coaches don't seem to know
Is that I can feel every blow.
The stars I see are not in space
They twinkle and burst in my face.

LOVE OF GAMES

There are some men who only strive
To engage in games all their lives.
They live in huge stately mansions
Unrestrained, can't keep their pants on.

Surrounded, by wild frantic fans,
The yield to wild dreamlike demands.
Their sparkling skills for certain games,
Earn them grand fortunes and broad fame.

Their minds void of positive things.
The feel that sports have made them kings.
They get away clean with neglect,
Thinking talents replace respect.

Their minds hold thoughts like little boys.
They feed on deafening crowd noise.
Games and parties are all they know,
Real life ain't real, it's just a show.

With little talent they savor,
And display brute-like behavior.
Though they're just plain ordinary
They see themselves as royalty.

So fast they rise, and fast they fall,
Their chosen games will take their all.
The many games that they must play.
Is reason why they go astray,

Unrealistic expectations,
Harbor deep intense temptations.
Physical virtues caste as skills,
Enhanced by illegal pills.

Playing the game, their only goal,
For victory they trade their souls.
Their keen childlike passion to win,
Voids their status as grownup men.

Can't expect them to be adult.
The games they love becomes their cult.
Maturity and reason fades,
Overwhelmed by relentless praise.

Their expressed love for all these games.
Illustrates some ultimate shame.
It's all unreal but they can't see.
These games are void of honesty.
In spite of all that's said and done,
These games are not played just for fun.

ANGRY PLAYERS

Busted lips and bleeding mouths,
They give to women who share their vows.
They don't leave it all on the field,
Or give dark spirits time to heal.

Their murky minds spin make believe,
Reality they can't achieve.
They brag about being he-men,
Yet, abuse defenseless women.

Protected by their fleeting fame,
They exert violence with no shame.
When player's wives cover black eyes,
Why are we so stunned and surprised?

Ladies are forced to share their lives
With men who make them battered wives.
Those men who cry at games they lose
Shed no tears for women they bruise.

These men who play these games for fun.
Can't shock us with mean things they've done.
Each time they score they jump for joy
Like little children with a toy.

Watching abusers play these games
Society must share some blame.
How much logic can we expect
From minds of men that go unchecked?

KEEPERS OF THE GOLD

I've been told that keepers of gold
Are a rare and hungry breed.
Faith only in what's bought and sold.
Their only religion is greed.

They cheat, lie, and make crooked deals,
And do it all at our expense.
They take pride in all they can steal,
And never offer a defense.

Truly spawns of demon seed,
They violate most every trust.
Always taking what they don't need,
All for them and nothing for us.

The keepers of the gold learn to lie
With an extreme dexterity,
And never give the truth a try
Their dreaded fear is poverty.

Blind greed and gluttony are their flaws.
They become our so-called leaders,
So they can dictate all the laws.
Then keep all the gold, and bleed us.

With no reverence for God or man,
Their conscience numb, as lies are told.
Their only fears are failing plans,
And losing portions of their gold.

Ignored are their many blessings,
Good character is never shown.
They measure worth by possessions,
And worship trinkets that they own.

They clutch tightly to their safe place,
While all the world is put on hold.
They always get to keep their space,
Along with all their precious gold.

They have no heart no love or soul,
And yet their gluttony prevails.
We watch these keepers of the gold,
And often pray their efforts fail.

YOU TALK TOO MUCH

Your empty words can fill a room,
Your hot air a million balloons.
You speak in loud and noisy waves,
Attacking ears with rants and raves.

Ears that can't take all your nonsense,
Soon shut down and go on defense.
Breaking silence with nothing to say,
Just puts your mouth on display.

You're anxious to put your spin on
Every topic with opinion.
Leave golden silence unbroken,
Just let some thoughts go unspoken.

You've got the scoop on every event,
 On Every subject you comment.
You never hear what's being said,
Because you have to talk instead.

When you desire to be heard,
Nothing can stop your gushing words.
Just when do you listen? Never!
Constant talk don't make you clever.

There's no one who can talk that much,
And not tell lies or stay in touch.
You talk so loud ears start to burn
No other speaker gets a turn.

And when there's nothing left to say,
You just keep talking anyway.
You talk on and on endlessly.
In your case speech should not be free.

You don't care if it's false or true,
Details and facts don't bother you.
Knowledge and truth just don't show up,
You'd never let them interrupt.

Others can't get past your loud voice,
so silence is their only choice.
You talk about things you don't know,
You let your lack of knowledge show.

You won't admit when you are wrong,
Each time you trip over your tongue.
You're void of thoughts and full of talk,
Those who hear you wish you would walk.

Talk, talk, talk, all about nothing.
Loud empty words are all you bring,
Talking louder than a choir can sing.
Yet your words have no truthful ring.

Let that useless rambling expire.
Don't think your words raise you higher.
Your tongue surely must burn like fire?
Your jaws should be ready to retire.

I won't tell you not to talk so much,
But I ask, would you PLEASE SHUTUP?

BRAGGING

Those tales you spin no doubt are stretched,
There's little truth in your word plays.
Somehow it seems it's all far-fetched,
When the air fills with such self-praise.

Your words flow like a dreaded force,
With your stories and boasting voice.
You test the load the nerves can take.
Can't you see we know you're a fake?

You might proclaim that jealousy,
Is why we doubt the words you say.
In those lies you tell constantly,
Veracity has gone astray.

Your words flow out in faulty streams.
The lies you tell you can't keep straight.
You then portray deceptive scenes,
With bogus lies that you create.

You take on the role of hero,
With lies that are too hard to sell.
You are the star in every show,
In every story that you tell.

Your silly stories are the worse,
You lie with unsound depiction.
Your descriptions are so diverse,
That sound reason voids your fiction.

The energy used to nurse bragging skills,
Renders precious time ripe to kill.
You're Dazed and confused void of will
In your maze of lies truth gets spilled.

EGO

A speck of dust, with too much pride
He dwells in places hard to reach.
Less than a drop in rivers wide.
Just grainy sand upon the beach.

Bloated egos be of sickness,
And the core of his self-esteem.
Some strange, toxic apparatus
Becomes a curse of foolish dreams.

The web of man's mighty ego
Entangle him in self-concern.
He swears there's nothing he can't know.
That blinds him to what he could learn.

He rides his ego and his luck,
And burns the truth within his fires.
His twisted thinking runs amuck,
And spawns the scourge of self-desires.

With every measure of success
His self-love grabs a tighter hold.
Now he's convinced that he's the best.
Such vision sees no truth that's told.

Such narcissism is so pure.
It jeopardizes harmony.
This rampant illness has no cure,
When ego has priority.

Glory and praise he can't resist,
Its bright splendor fulfills his need.
His foul behavior will persist,
On hungry cravings it will feed.

His blessings he fails to mention,
Instead he wears a hero's cape,
He clings to dreams and pretention,
As his reality escapes.

With all the things he's never done,
His self-worship is profane.
He's just a blip under the sun.
To think he's special is insane.

His smugness has become his art.
He fails to probe reality.
He won't accept that he's just a part
Of something much bigger than he.

THE GOOD GUYS

There is a lie bad boys have caste,
They claim that good guys finish last.
Those ladies who believe this myth
Get trapped in spells of boundless width.

This lie they tend to often tell
Will lure some ladies with its spell.
Enchanted by his brand of noise
They need to be with those bad boys

They sacrifice all style and poise,
In hopes to gain some greater joys.
Some ladies think these men have skills
To heighten bliss and give grand thrills.

While random passion steals their voice,
They let their hunger make that choice.
Sure they will thrill and delight you,
But those Good guys will excite you.

Sure Bad boys make you say yes
But Good Guys make you say yes yes.
Curiosity rules your mind,
You defy every warning sign.

You know his love you'll never share,
Yet you cling tight and just don't care.
Good guys will make you their mission.
Bad boys always come up missing.

You see loyalty as boring,
So bad boys you keep adoring.
Perhaps you're just exploring,
Looking for new ways of scoring.

You think his coarse intensity
Outweighs sound sensitivity.
They say that bad boys punch and bruise.
You say they are falsely accused.

But soon you learn they'll crush your dreams,
And take away your self-esteem.
Their Sympathy never in range.
Their brand of passion becomes strange.

They only count the heart they steal.
Their true self they'll never reveal.
You're no part of his future goals.
His vested interest you'll never hold

His treachery is common place.
He throws his dirt right in your face.
Soon you can only cry and scream
As sad tears fall in hearty streams.

You want a bad boy, be my guest.
You won't survive his grueling test.
Bad boys will never console you.
They seek only to control you.

With your black eyes and busted lips,
You'll never hold him in your grip.
And as he drifts to winds that shift.
Deep pain will be your final gift.
Pain is all that you can expect,
Because bad boys have no respect.

TEXTING AND DRIVING

Some drivers like to text and drive.
Reducing chances, they'll survive.
They can't keep their eyes on the road
Or remember the driver's code

So bored they turn their idle minds
To super phones that glow and shine.
They embrace their phones fancy chimes
While crossing over yellow lines.

They seem to have some deep passion
To send their useless expressions,
Across those wireless networks.
Faulty drivers becomes berserk.

Their useless gossip claims the day,
Their nonsense is put on display.
Their one track minds drift into dreams.
Distraction flows in steady streams.

Much idle texting fills their days.
They say nothing one million ways.
Their fancy phones are awesome toys,
Destined to cut some stranger's joys.

The roads they drive they just can't find
When they have texting on their mind.
Some senses seem to disappear,
When they text they fail to hear.

Precious time on idle chatter,
Spent on subjects that don't matter.
I worry that this newfound trance
Will grow to stages more advance.

Their heads fill with random ideas,
And discard all rational fears.
They caste those clear ideas from mind,
And make bad use of idle time.

Still they all continue to text,
And play games with their phone gadgets.
Messages no one needs to know,
Are sent forth with persistent flow.

Their hands hold in their possession
This instrument of obsession.
They love to send and receive
Yet somehow they don't perceive
The hidden dangers they create
Until they meet a tragic fate.

WHAT DO WE HAVE TO SING ABOUT

It's no big surprise
That Crime's on the rise
Rich men cheat and poor men steal
Poor men pay and rich men deal
It's unfair but time won't heal.

All reason has become absurd,
While taunting danger is the word.
Normal life comes with a high price,
And with each breathe we roll the dice.

There's a huge hole in our blue sky.
The world is mad and gone awry.
Mankind has now become a beast,
He's given up on hope and peace.
The doomsday clock has been reset
Causing more havoc and regret.

No peace is made when prideful fools
Make war and death its handy tools.
No good can come on battlefields,
Where nervous young men shoot to kill.

Perplexed Politicians cannot lead us:
They become richer as they bleed us.
They deceive us with the lies they feed us.
Deep in the sand their heads are stuck,
While human chaos runs amuck.

Eternal war is in motion.
Hatred flows like Oil floods oceans.
Because they have no clue or plan,
Leaders misuse their fellow man.

With no answers or emotions,
They hope for some Magic potions.
Seeking new contracts for their souls,
They've lost interest in common goals.

They waste time in useless huddles,
Pollution flows in sticky puddles.
Toxic fumes spreads in foul misuse,
Defacing nature with abuse.

Common people gripe and groan,
And fill the air with dirges and moans.
We can't change the world or change our doubts
So what do we have to sing about?

YOUNG HUSTLERS

He makes promises that seem impossible,
But fulfillments always come to pass.
His poised confidence disturbs me
As much as his dubious craft.

One eye is focus on the future,
He takes in sights that only he sees.
He monitors the present circumstances
Fixated on reality.

I watch him do that special dance.
He hears the sound of his own beat.
We hike to seek new excitement,
The steps we take become unique.

We're partners without enterprise,
Advancing forward without dreams.
His mind is working overtime,
He forges out a basic scheme.

He decides that we must treat ourselves
To a movie and a meal.
Being pragmatic I suggest:
That's impossible, unless we steal.

It seemed that he couldn't clearly see.
Movies and meals both cost money,
I remind him that we have none.
But he shrugs it off and struts proudly

"Just follow me and watch success."
Reluctantly I tag along,
But my mind tells me it's hopeless.
Most of all to me it feels wrong.

I know of his successful past,
I've seen his methods and his confidence,
"Mister could you spare a dime? He asks,
To adult strangers that we meet.

When Most respond positively.
 He flashes me a winning smile.
He shakes his change triumphantly,
"Got all this in half a mile."

"We got our show fare," he shouts,
And I felt a sense of relief,
From my discomfort and my doubt.
Eleven year-olds hustling change
Was so uncool and scary strange.

To my dismay he continued his quest.
I didn't understand his logic.
"Come on man just give it a rest
We can relax now we got this."

"We got show fare, that's good," he says.
"But we still got a mile to go.
We'll want some popcorn and sodas
To snack on while watching the show."

CLOUDED IDENTITY

They seek and search in hope to find
Some scrap of proof and peace of mind.
Souls of shady identity,
Ever wishing what cannot be.

Their Vacuous and haunting needs
Command that passion that they seek.
They know too well that deep desire
Must be exposed or must expire.

From drowning dreams they surge to light
Those goals that disappeared from sight,
Intent and function never meek,
With strength and purpose it shall seek.

With all its dangers and its risk,
Some truth and passion will be missed.
Deep down inside they seek some part,
But stays aloof to spare their heart.

Truth can't be heard that make no sound
Love can't be lost if never found
Trust is masked when lies are spoken
Love has passed when hearts are broken.

I REMEMBER WHEN

I remember when angry crazy people
Were committed to asylums and given proper treatment,
Not given national recognition,
Book deals and their own television shows.

I remember when people talked to
The person in the same room,
Not captivated and spellbound
By the voice on their wireless phones

I remember when movies were pleasant,
Yet held drama and hilarity, and
Didn't have caution signs and warnings,
gratuitous pornography, foul language,
And horrid blood streams.

I remember when the pursuit of love was good,
And something every soul felt they deserved,
Not something that required misinterpretation, criminal
accusations, and restraining orders.

I remember when neighbors cared,
And when people enjoyed being with families,
And weren't ever seeking escape routes,
Alone time, and peace of mind.

When people would lend a helping hand,
Or a sympathetic ear, and would greet
Each other with provocative interest,
Warm smiles and kind words.

I remember when people were cheerful
And accepting of each other's style.
They never gazed at strangers with
Suspicious stares, or gross mistrust.

I remember general conversations where
Everyone listened to everyone else's words.
I remember when I remember when adults and kids
played different games, and were not intrigued by high
scores, blinking lights, and amusing noises.

I remember when music consisted of lyrics being sung,
Instead of loud noise, foul language, and verbal abuse
From thuggish broods, masquerading as angry artists,
With no recourse but to shout in negative tones,
As they flaunted their checkered past.

I remember when people's level of fear
Didn't rise at the thought of unlocked doors,
At the sight of Loitering teenagers,
And the sound of distant exploding firecrackers.

I remember when people didn't have to
Check in their closets, look under their beds,
And take inventory of their possessions
Each time they return to their homes.
Unfortunately, no one else remembers and most wish
That I would forget.

OPEN MIC

Wouldn't it be special if there was a place
Where poets could meet face to face,
And Spend quality time together,
With poem after poem of whatever.

To tell stories they had to tell,
Or spin some yarns and cast some spell
Wouldn't that be special?
And wouldn't it be special if,
This was the best place to go,
Where Poets could stand in a row,
And let their verses and images flow?

A place where verses ran free or rhyme,
Where every poet is allowed time
To express their own creation,
Spawn from active imaginations.

Wouldn't it be special
To hear the things both good and bad
That the mind has conjured up to share.
Where the atmosphere reeks of cheer,
And poets were ecstatic to be there,
To feel this sweet poetic kiss.
What a joy it would be if such a place exists?

A special place where no one wore a judge's cloak,
But listened in earnest to the words you spoke.
No sentence are you convicted of,
Just those you are convicted to,
Those that ring out in verses with love.

Where we could forget the outside world,
And get together to feel joy and all its remnants,
That appear each time we convene,
To enhance our intense sensibilities.

Where people enjoyed listening as much as speaking,
Where everyone would feed from the pool of creativity,
As it is presented collectively.
Where swollen egos and arrogance
Meet defeat at the hands of tolerance.

Where intimidation and trepidation
Has hopped the train and left the station.
Where sweet and sour thoughts
Are crafted into forms of art.
And souls of congenial interest
Share the splendor of their verses.

Where minds find new paths and take new chances
To learn a novel range of steps and dances.
Where rhythms once beyond imagination
Becomes clear because of determination.

Wouldn't it be sublime if there was a place that could
Instill an abundant wealth of inspiration
To encourage profound motivation,
And promote enough insightful imaginations
To negate the ubiquitous proclivity
For desultory procrastination?
Wouldn't that be nice?
I think so.

DAMAGED GOODS

I think I know who wrecked me,
In fact, I'm sure I do,
But I'm supposed to forgive them
The way good Christians do.

I don't know if that is possible.
I can say the words like others do,
But that doesn't mean they're true.
And It's hard for me to be a hypocrite.

I'm sure they cause my lack of confidence.
I want to forgive and make myself whole,
But I'm not sure I can let things go.
I was hurt and abused by the weak and confused.

In ways that were rude, in ways that were crude.
They were pleased to inflict
Harsh attitudes and foul moods,
Then found knowledge easy to refuse.

I know who made Intimidation
And made trepidation my foundation,
Who cause constipation of ideas
With their excessive restriction and trivial friction.
That reduced my self-expressions,
Then took my voice to silence.

A vile petty character with limited ambition,
Erased my self-worth and sense of value.
Because my genius was suppressed
By tribulations and blindness.

I think I know who spoiled me
In a way that was not so good.
My goals were void and askew, off course
And criticized as moronic and worthless.

I Know I know who tried to ruined me
with accepted delusion of self-made perceptions.
Then held me hostage to duress.
In their mirrors they saw perfection.

I cannot escape the mental chains
That still create storms in my brain
And stir those raging migraines,
That set me on a path of gloom.

I know who wrecked me,
Ruined me, spoiled me, and wounded me,
But I guess I'll never know
Who did the same to them.

Or why they had the need, the urge
And the intentions to do it to me.
Yes, I know who wrecked me, but fortunately
They didn't destroy me, and I am renewed
Refurbished, rebuilt and upgraded.

SECRET CRUSH

She greets the wind with graceful strides.
Her voice sings even when she talks.
Her head held high with poise and pride.
Her beauty hovers where she walks.

Her image fills my happy eyes.
This new bliss my senses have found,
My spirit shout out joyous cries.
I'm captivated and I'm bound.

She lends her grace to cloudless nights
Lasting goodness must be her goal,
She incites joy in new daylight,
Her eyes reveal the purest soul.

She's in balance with perfection,
Her presence brings a blissful glow.
She has no need for correction,
She is the star of every show.

She turns the saddest day to fun.
She's an endless energy flow
Her radiance powers the sun.
Angels envy her I know.

She's more than just a pretty face:
With great beauty her soul is touched.
Sheltered inside her body's space,
Is mass enchantment she has clutched.

As she strides with artful splendor
The air she touches lingers sweet.
The earth beneath her surrenders
And hug the arches of her feet.

Elated are those witnesses
Who see her spark the air with fire.
Her grace and polished loveliness
Tames all spirits wildest desires.

Her image seen in angels' dreams,
She's a rare and delicate mold.
Her beauty is so seldom seen.
Her splendor spreads and then unfolds.

Her presence spells sheer poetry.
She gives my heart a special feel.
Even skeptics can plainly see,
Her spirit is special and real.

WISH I WERE SUPERMAN

I wish that I were Superman
Each time I gaze upon your face.
It seems to me no mortal man
Could hope to share your grace.

If I could be a superman,
Then I would have a fighting chance.
With you I'd share a super plan,
Along with hope for true romance.

But I'm not him, I can't compete.
My efforts fall like sad echoes.
Compared to him I'm frail and weak,
In awe, I live in his shadow.

His power is limitless; he's built to last.
He knows just how to fly and flash.
He thrills us as he streaks and dash,
Roaring by with a cosmic blast.

I Can't break the barrier of sound,
 Or speed past bullets as they sink.
Can't flash past jets above the ground,
Can't circles the world in a blink.

Can't streaks across the clear blue sky
To places where no eagles soar.
Or hear the brisk wind's mighty sigh,
Past the sound of the jet engine's roar.

He'll grace the sky flying around.
Earth born and bound and here I stand.
My feet stay firmly on the ground.
But if I were Superman,

I would meet your expectations.
Be on your page and up to speed,
Meet every qualification.
And be everything you will need.

I would fly across the cosmos
And go to worlds past anywhere.
And gather gifts you deserve most,
So you can hold those treasures near.

I'd fill your days with happiness.
And seek my riches in your charms.
You'd be my joyous treasure chest.
I'd keep you safe and in my arms,

I'd ascend to the highest goals
So your wishes I could serve
I would turn dark lump of coals
Into those diamonds you deserve

But I'm not even Clark Kent,
And I don't have super strength.
But if I'm ever in a fight,
I won't be stopped by Kryptonite.

DIAMOND IN THE ROUGH

He had a sound and gentle heart,
But got a faulty shattered start,
Seeking delicacies from waste cans
Was his survival's master plan.

Misery was a constant theme,
That dealt harsh blows and splintered dreams.
He struggled for the things he got,
Life never offered him a lot.

The things he got he had to take,
Because he never got a break.
To live sometimes he broke the law.
But I don't see that as a flaw.
He never took or asked for much,
Or sought frills that luxury touched.

Misfortune, never passed him by,
It always stopped to catch his eye.
Bad luck was his constant friend,
But he broke that bond in the end.

He had a set determined mind,
And some happiness he did find.
In spite of constant toil and strife,
He did find comfort in this life.

HERO WORSHIP

Heroes have holes its plain to see.
They are as broken as you and me.
They've never really save the day,
 Though some feel it happened that way.

With focused views and minds in shape
We know they don't wear masks or capes.
In glory they shall never bask,
Or volunteer for gallant task.

And even though they lose some fights,
It's not because of Kryptonite.
They haven't solve a single crime,
Or even have such thoughts in mind.

They haven't caught any villains,
Or prevented serial killings.
 And unexpressed emotions hide.
Wounded hearts that are filled with pride

We know they are not perfect, and yet
We find it easy to forget.
They have special ailments and needs,
We can't define the ways they bleed.

We never paint these men as weak,
Or point out their faults when we speak.
Yet hero worship is soon destroyed
When heroic feats become void.
They are just humans with normal lives.
Some make mistakes some cheat on wives.

We give much praise and admiration
To those who earn commendation.
Emotions change without a pause
If we suspect they've broken laws.

We quickly focus on their flaws
Then attack with sharpened claws.
As Praises fade like windblown dust,
We strip them of hero's status.

Hero's prestige is placed in doubt,
And crowds shift ways they yell and shout.
Just can't seem to not be needing.
Just can't seem to stop the bleeding.

Locked in silence and dire needs,
Aching hearts make wounded pleas.
Those holes that these heroes all bear
Are noticed only when we care.

HONEST POLITICIANS

Honesty in politicians
Is something that remains a joke.
They have far too much ambition,
And many schemes to get your vote.

A thousand ways they find to lie,
With subtle smirks that make me wince.
For reasons that I know not why,
Their slick words leave me unconvinced.

They show fake personalities,
Because they have none of their own.
They play upon our sympathies,
Yet slow they morn but quick they moan.

White lies and empty promises
Are but scams and tricks of their trade.
And in the face of compromise
The truth is like a ghost that fades.

Members of this restricted guild
Will lie, cheat and manipulate.
Their objective, to shape your will
With cons that they initiate.

Their party has no mirth or song,
They find themselves not having fun.
This group to which they all belong,
 Sanction the lies of all who run.

Their sleep comes trouble free at night,
Because they are a perverse kind.
Their wallets always full and tight.
Remote from guilt of common minds.

They show concerned only for fame,
And just how right they make things look.
Their fond wish is to locked their name,
 And their role in history books.

They continue to fight and fight,
For things they just can't justify.
They have no plan to make things right,
And so they continue to lie.

WHY DO MY DOGS LIKE YOU?

I know I don't have all the facts.
With you my dogs are too relaxed.
Maybe I'm having illusions.
Maybe I'm full of confusion.

When you pet them the get frisky,
With anyone else that's risky.
The fact that they're so overjoyed,
Makes me suspicious and annoyed.

And what I just can't understand,
Why they growl and chase the mailman,
Someone they see most every day,
But with you, they just want to play.

These dogs are ferocious and mean,
Yet are pleased when you're on the scene.
There's something going on here,
That has become my biggest fear.

Some one's hiding something from me.
Under my eyes that I can't see?
I hate being so suspicious.
But Deception is malicious.

My crazy thoughts might be nonsense,
Just my own Imagined suspense.
Yet, I am lost and unconvinced.
And my dark thoughts still make me wince.

My dim views are so upsetting.
With these messages I'm getting.
My dogs are too happy and content
Whenever they're in your presence.

It's become a dark mystery
Why they treat you better than me.
I don't mean to be pathetic
But what I see I don't get it
So I must ask you once again
Why are my dogs now your best friends?

I OWE MYSELF AN APOLOGY

For taking the punishment I didn't deserve,
Forced to honor and serve.
Then follow the drifting majority
Forced to cater and bow and not be me.

I apologize for doubting my status,
Thinking that I was below my station,
For absorbing the unfair scorn,
For Self-esteem so dearly mourned.

I will no longer rebuke myself
For the failing s of someone else,
For thinking I shouldn't make mistakes,
Or never be tricked by what's fake.

The world is pretty much the same,
Families assume different names,
Giving lies a grand reception
To set the stage for deception.

Weaving lies to be believed,
Secure only when they deceive.
Like flocks of comics poised to please.
 Onlookers laughing up their sleeves.

I apologize for thinking that
I must show blind trust
To those who find abuse a must.
Betrayal fills their icy hearts,
And squander hope before it starts.

I apologize for telling myself that it's my fault
That dad didn't stay, just had to vault.
I owe me an apology
For ever apologizing needlessly,
Or thinking someone was better than me,
Because they claimed it endlessly.

I owe myself an apology for my silence,
For thinking my thoughts made no sense.
Real solutions are easily lost
When dead silence becomes the cost.

And no solution can be found
When your thoughts make no earthly sounds.
When silence is left unbroken
You can gain no force no focus.

I apologize for not liking me well enough
 To keep some things to myself,
For believing that thinking was a trap,
Instead of a great escape.

For walking in circles searching for a hero;
A hopeless task as we all know,
When all the time my eyes couldn't see
The hero I sought dwelled inside me.

AMAZING ME

When I gave you what you ask me for
It left us both sad and up upset.
You always wanted even more,
You were a master at regret.

I once held you in high esteem.
I thought you possessed dignity.
You were my prize and lifelong dream.
You made me laughed out constantly.

your succulent lips invite me to dine.
Your spirits lift expectations.
I drink your presence like tasteful wine,
And offer sound dedication.

Your grandeur elevates the air,
And how I long to kiss those lips.
Your touch I would die to share
And feel orgasmic fingertips.

Your sweet skin bears a magic touch.
Your image brings hunger and thirst.
Bewildered lust will slaughter pride.
Enlightenment makes the darkness fade.
It become clear where light resides.
Clear focus takes away the shade.

Each time we engage and carress
The truth was there but I missed it
I bathed in your loving senses,
But its meaning my mind dismissed.

When I found the righteous path,
I finally conquered my lust spell.
I steer away from evils wrath,
And all those lies I heard you tell

With myself I'm so amazed,
No doubt you became offended.
And I will give me proper praise,
Now that my blindness has ended.

PLANET EARTH

Ever constant in its wonder,
Ever present to be plundered.
Unfeasible cloaked secrets
Holds damaged dreams within regret.

She's host to every kind of life,
While hanging adrift in deep space.
Amidst and endless universe,
This lonely planet known as earth.

We take for granted this great gift,
As reasons sours and justice shifts.
Firm stark closeness is never found,
Where dark forces tightly surround.

The vastness that touch forever,
Is unapproached and all alone.
Urgent knowledge we need to grasp,
To rescue our dear island home.

We're grounded by its gravity,
We'll never solve its mystery.
Each day becomes its history,
As we confront its blind journey.

TRIBAL SKINS

The flowing of the universe,
Prolongs mortal man's deadly curse.
Hate becomes bold while love grows cold,
And with that, everything gets worse.

It drives sane men to insane deeds,
And spark dark urges they don't need.
All charity is put on hold,
When reason dies, chaos controls.

Cowards ponder ways to mask it,
Dreamers think we have surpassed it.
We have no winning songs to sing,
When gloom and hate waits in the wings.

It's clear now that we must face this,
The sign was clear but it was missed.
We lost it in a blurring twist.
Man's mass compassion was dismissed.

He held racism with a clutch,
Using excuses as a crutch.
In each dark heart is where it lives,
Hatred is all it has to give.

With some men compelled to believe
The tone of the skin he received,
Indicates superior genes,
And knowledge the world hasn't seen.

Weak unworthy men embrace it,
Men with hopes and dreams erase it.
At times it's hard to discuss it;
Heated banter can't be trusted.
Because some men snub those in pain,
Their comments are expressed in vain.

THE SNOB

They've convinced no one but themselves,
That they are impressive and grand.
Riding hard on their high horses,
Across those acres of stolen land.

From pedestals they don't look down.
They love the warmth of the spotlight.
So out of touch and off the ground,
They blocked obvious clues from sight.

Their need to be superior,
Allows no room to budge or flinch.
With heads lodged in posteriors,
They assent to their royal stench.

They justify foolish pleasures
By cataloging it as style.
They think class is measured
By the height of their money piles.

Their muzzle so far in the air
They can't keep the road in focus.
They'll never share, they'll never care,
So they choke on private vapors.

SENSELESS THINGS

Broken wires and flat spare tires.
Silly rules that everyone breaks.
Brash people with cell phones rage
Talking loud with nothing to say.
They talk to command center stage

Those privileged men who break laws,
Are elected to make our laws.
People who laugh when things aren't funny.
Rich people afraid to spend their money.
Politicians with no mission,
Only out for recognition.

Timid people who watch and scream
At scary movies on the screen.
People who are starving to death,
While we waste abundant wealth.

Wages that start to fade from sight,
While prices soar to endless heights.
Enchanted fans who idolizes
Special skills of regular guys.

Silent letters we never use
It makes spelling hard and confused.
They're only there to take up space.
They're odd and awkward, out of place.

Good girls who love bad boys.
Grown men intrigued by toys.
People who shoot drugs in their arm,
Seeking bliss in dreamlike charm.

People who don't seem to know,
That they have little skills to show.
Always ready to rant and rave
For instant access to the stage.

Pretty people in camouflage,
Unyielding faith in a mirage.
Two story dwellings with no stairs.
Insecure billionaires.

Breathing nicotine instead of air.
Talking to people who aren't there.
Thinking pit bulls are passive pet.
Cursing at your television set.
Expecting leadership from the blind.
Seeking logic from a senseless mind.

People awarded some prize unearned,
Like this president and a first term.
They claim that justice is for all,
Yet, the guilty rich will never fall.

RECONNECTION

Distant paths find vague dignity
In dark places we seldom see.
Fellowship and Congregation
Brings brotherhood to completion.

We're as different as night and day,
Yet our like parts flow the same way.
We're so much alike that it's perverse,
Yet so different our flows reverse.

Our diversities blend and merge,
Our consistency bend and purge,
Our gathered spirits mix and surge.
Together we all feel the urge.

Those who continue looking back
Sometimes get trampled in their tracks.
So cast aside all haunting wrath
That makes you walk a twisted path.

When someone feels sadness somewhere,
Some distant eyes one tear could spare.
While joyful eyes hold tears and mist
Open hearts will soothe vague distress.,

Stop for a second and behold,
The things we have, worth more than gold.
From the strength of our work and thoughts
To all the help good friends have brought.

Tell me something I have said,
That you never thought to say,
Or some move I have made,
That you did a different way.

Listen to the beats on every level
Reject the deceit of spiteful devils
We must pick up the pace for peace,
And share humanity at least.
We are one and no one can hide
Forget these traps we know as pride

Before you're ready to dismiss,
All this talk as ignorant bliss,
Banish all wasted memories.
Allow thoughts that resolve and please.
Forget past beliefs that left you twisted.
Find your good and revisit.

REAL BEAUTY

They say that beauty is only skin deep,
But you have it all covered.
Yours is more than just pretty skin,
It's the essence of what's within.

No doubt you have a perfect smile
Accompanied by its radiance,
A perfect smile that brings the sun,
Reversing frowns with joyous fun.

Spellbound and uncontrolled by choice,
Attuned Vibrations find some course.
Your actions tell me your story.
It's plain to see you seek no glory.

You have no games or secret things.
Your worth is in the joy you bring.
Your presence bans all signs of gloom.
Laughter still lingers in your room.

Your laughter makes your essence glow.
Then spills the joy and lets it flow.
I am willing to take a chance,
On days you do your happy dance.

ODE TO MY GUITAR

Your six strings play a billion songs.
At times I'm forced to sing along,
Casting out my inhibitions,
Making you my only mission.

You attract beguile and tempt me,
Your curves beckon seductively.
You are the prize of all my toys.
I love the purr of your sweet noise

You entice me to pluck your strings,
Then allure me to dance and sing.
I feel this need to pick and strum,
I feel Compelled to sing and hum.

Sometimes you bring me fantasies,
Then play them out with perfect ease.
Your mellow sounds are amazing,
I'm always awed, always praising.

Because your music flows within.
I often wear a happy grin.
Your solid equanimity,
Constantly find the best of me.

I love your shape, your riffs and runs,
Your splendid art transforms to fun.
With melodies you play so well,
You fill my ears with peaceful spells

I banish all unhappy glum,
Each time I pick you up to strum.
You leave me ever satisfied,
Your music nurtures thrills and pride.

I touch your strings and I can trace,
Contagious smiles upon my face.
Our unique bond and special touch
Forge ties that hold tight in a clutch.

I pick your strings, caress your curves,
But I will never pluck your nerves.
Though I fondle you constantly,
I know you'll never tire of me.

SOMEDAY

Someday perhaps there'll come a time
When wicked sinners all repent,
And evil thoughts are never spent,
When foul contempt turns to respect,
And men no longer hold neglect.

Someday perhaps there'll come a time
When ignorance becomes extinct,
And mindless fools will learn to think,
When wicked deeds are left behind,
And hatred cease to rule the mind.

Someday perhaps there'll come a time
When selfish thieves no longer take,
And tender hearts no longer break,
When inner goodness men restore,
And evil deeds become a bore.

Someday perhaps there'll come a time
When vicious violence is erased,
And kindness becomes commonplace,
When hatred fails to wear a mask,
And men longer worship cash.

Someday perhaps there'll come a time
When men forsake their wilder side,
And self-control becomes their guide,
And bad men, just for goodness sake
Seek forgiveness for cruel mistakes.

Although it's not reality,
Perhaps someday it just might be,
But for now we can only pray,
That there will come a time, some day.

SUCCESS

A job well done brings deep delight
Success is when you get it right.
Deep cravings is the essence
Of the outcome you present.

Success is found not in world fame
Or fortunes by another name.
Both wear a phony fancy face,
Neither one has a solid base.

Success comes with self-contentment,
And enjoyment of achievement.
Can't crave the need to be a star,
For it will come with who you are.

It's not one lone definition,
But mutual recognition.
Men are made of complexities,
A fragile blend of recipes.

Success combines essential need,
In proper time, at proper speed.
With good reasons to rise and shine,
progressive thoughts will hold the mind.

It brings great purpose to one's deeds,
It sanctions hope, while soothing greed.
It provides sound concrete projects,
And brings resolve to all efforts.

No rewards or bonus do you need
Or prizes for outstanding deeds
It gives up worth and sustains pride,
To lead the way and be a guide.

You're satisfied with its essence
To create strong stoic substance.
It's the thing that's done the best
When there's progress in the process.

Complications far from mind,
Competition left behind,
Rewards that come with your efforts,
Are bonuses unexpected.

BITTERSWEET

Sweet as honey there you were,
I saw you as the perfect mate.
But slick and sly was your legacy
Like a nasty snake you bit me.

Your ice cold heart, too hard to thaw,
You were evil untamed and raw.
With you there was no way to win.
You represented walking sin.

Your sweet look only goes to waste,
With unsuspected bitter taste.
Dollar signs replaced your heart,
It was obvious from the start.

I was struck blind and could not see,
Your sly deception conquered me.
But soon I saw your sweetness fade
Inside you dwell dark gloomy shades

Soon I could see that your main flaw,
Was an ice cold heart I could not thaw.
Sly as a fox evil as a snake,
Your bad habits you cannot shake.

TAKING THINGS FOR GRANTED

Taking things for granted,
They expect more than they deserve.
Expecting all debts to be paid.
And granted some wishes unmade.

They feel some grand entitlement,
And acknowledge no set limits.
They have the urge to spread their wings
To gather all and everything.

The more they own the more they crave,
With possessions they rant and rave.
Their needs are more than their wants,
They like to stand up tall and flaunt.

They can never deal with the truth.
They shun all evidence and proof.
When greed proceeds with steady pace,
Limits are much too hard to face.

Their bland hearts ever set adrift,
They've come to expect unearned gifts.
They seek only what comes with ease,
And somehow they are never pleased.

To sound reason they become blind,
As thoughts of glitter steal their minds.
Silver spoons and silver platters
Are the things to them that matter.

TEMPTATION

When I hear your sweet laughter loom,
My hidden passions reach full bloom.
Gazing upon your fragile face
Makes me long to invade your space.

Your natural grace and easy stride,
Makes me humble, forsaking pride.
Although I'm king in your presence,
Apart from you I' m a peasant.

Each day I'm captured in your glow,
My reckless thoughts flourish and grow.
I know somehow I must forget.
Yet I stand ready to submit.

The only way you'll wear my ring
Is if I forsake everything.
Can't help but feel that I've been cursed
Because I failed to meet you first.

I shouldn't have such impure thoughts,
But I'm human and full of faults.
My restless mind I must dissuade,
Then make these potent feelings fade.

I seek the valor to resist,
My surrender would be remiss.
I know it's wicked to want you
But I just don't know what to do.

I shake whenever I'm near you,
Not because I dread or fear you,
Mainly I feel that maybe I,
Might be compelled to cheat, then lie.

My delight must remain hidden.
My elation is forbidden.
Though my feelings grow strong and wide,
I vow to hold them deep inside.

My heart swells with great temptation.
I vibrate with palpitations,
But I'll pay my obligation,
And remain here at my station,
With logic and dedication.

I abandon all persistence,
And I vow to keep my distance.
Although I'll never forget you,
Your love I'll no longer pursue.
It's just the right thing to do.

THE LOST SOULS OF ABORTIONS

The lost souls of abortion drift.
Deprived of life, this precious gift
Oblivious to all they'll miss,
Sucked into some separate abyss.

We know not if they suffer pain.
These victims of the inhumane.
They disappear like drops of rain,
Summons to some gloomy domain.

Never to know their human worth,
They find death before they find birth.
Detached from troubled mothers' wombs,
They're banished to vast boundless tombs.

Unformed hopes vanish in a flash,
One chance for life then lost and passed.
This fragile life is harsh enough,
It's grim when it's unwanted stuff.

Never to be that blessed event.
All potential is lost and spent.
No laughter will they ever hear.
No concepts of love hate or fear.

Those mislaid souls will never blend,
For their beginning is their end.
Because of some grave decision.
New formed hearts never find rhythm.

No passion pleas or helping hands,
Just rapid destruction plans.
Innocence that need protection,
Betrayed and claimed by rejection.

Would-be existence becomes void
With horrid ways lives get destroyed.
We pray and hope somehow they'll find
Some place somewhere some peace of mind.

Perhaps out there some golden rays
Will shine some light on their dark days.
In some place those lost souls will play,
And stroll along the Milky Way.

THE ABYSS

We escape the womb just to see,
That earth is our last boundary.
Hearts and souls are held tight and close,
With wild vibrations as their host.

There is a joyful and pleasant
Nocturnal abyss that's present.
It gathers senses that emerge,
It makes emotions rise and surge.

The energy flow will fill you.
In ways both strange and familiar
Such surging energy runs through me,
And shines light on all that's gloomy.

Brings forth light for eyes to feast,
And steal some needed inner peace.
Its share beauty and resilience,
Brings forward its sparkling brilliance.

It opens up the mind and soul,
And brings forth new ideas to hold.
It maps a new and joyous route,
To the world void of stress and doubt.

Presenting sound concepts on time
Will bring profound ideals to mind.
This light I am supposed to know
Will then begin to spread its glow.

Help polish every bit and piece
To edit out this inner beast.
Keep dignity alive and well,
In hope to catch a lesser hell.

Its dubious power is in question
Its flaws and faults hold and press on.
A species prone to self-destruction
Has no place in new construction.

Clueless power will hold our fate,
When doors are locked with no escape.
Men will lose the will to explore,
When they resolve problems with war.

THE BOSTON TEA PARTY

In the harbor was a party.
Costly tea would go no farther.
No invitation was required,
Defiant causes were admired.

And all those uninvited guest,
Brought rebel spirits to object.
With hearty feelings on the rise,
Their gripes were made while in disguise.

Dressed like renegade Indian chiefs,
They spill tea to protest their beef.
Their actions made it very clear,
Revolution was drawing near.

Years deprived of contentment.
Years of collective resentment.
Has driven their anger to the brink,
To mix some tea no one would drink.

These men were angered and unpleased,
As they spilled those premium teas.
No sweet aroma or sweet taste;
Fine British tea they chose to waste.

They cared not for consequences,
And did not come to mend fences.
They felt that they had had enough,
The time had come so they got rough.

When they finally broke their silence.
Their restraint transformed to violence,
Thrown overboard were tons of tea,
That drift into the night lit sea.
Patriotism lurked in the breeze,
Rebellious minds felt soothed and pleased.

TRIBUTE TO THE BUS DRIVER

Like wingless planes that do not fly,
There is no soaring or glamour,
No open air, no clear blue sky,
Just high pitched screeching and clamor.

We drive obscure and bouncing paths.
We neither conquer or explore.
We seek escape from constant wrath,
From angry strangers at our door.

Bizarre expressions shape their face,
And sometimes put us I'll at ease.
Their flowing complaints have no base,
We doubt if they are ever please.

There seems to be hidden envy,
And they all swear we got it made.
They think our jobs are too easy,
And It's a crime that we get paid.

These outsiders just cannot grasp,
And they will never understand,
The mental anguish of this task,
Or the pressures that it demands.

Hard pressed as a horse drawn wagon
Each day we ride this dreary track.
This bus just rattles and drags on
It's even harder when it's packed.

Some days we only pick up fools,
And we must be prepared to deal
With people out to break the rules
And disregard the way we feel.

Other days also take their toll
In traffic that refuse to yield.
At times some drivers moves are bold,
They make the roads a battlefield.

A car speeds up to block the lane,
The driver knows we need to change.
Just for spite he's being a pain,
Just to keep us out of range.

Though praise is lost and out of place,
We can't forget that we're the host.
No one seems to note our grace.
"Thank you" are foreign words to most;

Some people seem so harsh and blind.
That loud drunk just won't take his seat,
Cell phone users crossing the line.
Profanity rings out on beat,

Loud preachers whose sermons are fake.,
Those who'll flash an invalid pass.
No one notes the efforts we make,
Or how hard our given task.

To us this comes as no surprise
We've driven long enough to know
That hostile attitudes arise,
Each time we have to stop then go.

THE ENCHANTED DISCONNECT

They speak only to what they clutch.
All conversation that they spend,
Seems to avoid the personal touch.
They speak wireless to distant friend.

Their eyes are blurred by what they hear,
Modern invention is to blame.
They fail to greet those standing near.
Their every word and thought is claimed.

They seem to seek some enchantment,
As they blur the path of reality.
They lose track of time that's spent,
The tool they hold is all they see.

Reality slips past their touch.
It seems as if they have no choice,
Their phone becomes their new life crutch.
They share words with a distant voice,

The personal touch becomes the price,
This new obsession has no end.
Mirth and laughter are sacrificed,
Saved only for long unseen friends.

Ears are focused but eyes are blind.
Attention is so far away,
And captivates many good minds.
Such rude neglect now rules the day.

Its novel intoxication
Seems to instill some sense of clout.
Logic escapes this addiction,
And follows the blind path of doubt.

So lost and enchanted by their cell
So unaware of their reflex.
They are empty shells in a spell
Engrossed in their mass words and text.

HARVEY AND IRMA

They brought us terror and bad dreams,
This nightmare wind destructive team.
From the murky shadows they walked,
Audacious and angry they stalked.

Deadly winds with no direction.
Focus on loss and destruction.
Pulling power lines to the ground,
And bringing bedlam all around.

They rummaged through the neighborhood,
Upsetting everything that stood.
Our peaceful world shivered and shook,
They never took a second look.

Their widespread random cruelty
Destroy things dear to so many.
With no regard for health or age,
They unleashed untamed windswept rage.

They instigated violence,
And captured us all with suspense.
Their shocking ire unjustified,
They didn't care who lived or died.

With Relentless anger they attacked,
And left destruction in their track.
Their anger had one single phase;
They gave no one honor or praise.

Their blind wrath was inflexible,
Merciless and insensible.
Catastrophe was their project,
Devastation was their logic.

Free from responsibility,
They left behind calamity.
Because their short lives had no joy,
Their main mission was to destroy.

Intensely seeking new subjects,
Mass destruction was their object.
They scheme to make more rivers rise,
While drowning out prayers and cries.

They move on to other places,
Stealing smiles from happy faces.
Their whistling winds bellow and boast,
While streaking swiftly up the coast.

WRITER'S BLOCK

Deep thoughts that once dwelled inside me
Now need some spell to set them free.
To Mr. Writer's block I pray
Clear this path that blocks my way.

Thoughts that are usually in my face,
Are lost in fog out there in space.
But thoughts would not confront my mind.
Concepts and Ideas were hard to find,

I feel the chains of frustration
That sends thoughts to oblivion.
Stress haunts my vain cogitations,
Inane is my concentration.

Though I had so much to convey,
But random thoughts chose to stay away.
Eloquent words I once could say
Vanished along with yesterday.

No sound ideas can I command.
I can form no sample or plan.
I've lost the use of my mental tools,
Exploration no longer at hand.

My inner thoughts and profound prose is
Dead as petals of winter roses,
They scamper to vast shifting winds,
Where dying sparks and limp thoughts end.

Stifled couplets, refuse to come.
Plots are toppled before they're spun.
Held captive are rhythms and rhymes,
With stress that lingers on my mind.

I dread my brain's lack of progress,
Of things I need most to express,
Sense and logic I need to touch,
So firm ideas my brain can clutch.

Dark frustration becomes the cost
Of writing talent, I have lost.
Ideas that once came easily,
Have now found ways to avoid me.

Such detachment is persistent.
Thoughts have become strange and distant.
My mind finds no creative birth
To lines of sweet unmeasured mirth.

My writer's face has lost its smile
For my sound prose is now exiled
My seeds of ideas are in shock,
Because of Mr. Writer's block.

WE'RE NOT OLD
w/ Delroy Simmons

We're not that old, our hair is just grey.
This grey comes not from passing time.
We're not lame, we just walk that way.
Because we left so much behind.

Once we made orderly protest
For human rights and decent jobs,
That was turned into a real mess,
We got tagged as a ruthless mob.

You picked a fight and breached our rights,
Your German Sheppard broke our skin.
Those vicious dogs you trained to kill.
You took command of man's best friend,
And made him hostage to your will.

Your pressure hoses sprayed us down,
No doubt this gave you much delight.
You clubbed and beat us to the ground,
Because we asked for human rights.
Yet you can't see why we are gray,
Or figure why we walk this way.

We can't depend on anyone
For fairness we think we deserve.
We have to get our own job done,
Because no one else has the nerve.

We're not grouchy, just not content.
We're still young with our shades of gray,
Even though our walk is slightly bent,
We're still sturdy walking this way.

We're not super and we're not weak.
We're not lazy, just tired and drained.
And equal justice we strongly seek,
In spite of blows that caused past pain.

We pray these rights will never fade
When politics become too bold.
No chord is struck that might dissuade
Modern youth to wither and fold.

Still you wonder why our hair is gray.
It's because we fought the battles.
And you wonder why we walk this way.
It's because we feel the rattles.
We're not cripple because we sway,
We're not old because strands are grey.

EVOLUTION

Locked in the prisons of the womb,
My anxieties trumped the gloom
That trail me like serene soldiers,
In search of a place for posers.

If I had known my coming fate,
I would have had the sense to wait,
But life has never worked like that.
We only think after we act.

I held tight but I still blew it.
Success vanished before I knew it.
I tackled many endless tasks,
Without glory in which to bask,

I sought its vast enlightenment,
In search of its pure excitement.
It brought fun, laughter and chatter,
Which is all that really matters.

In the glow of all victories,
I overcame sound tragedies.
Curiosity serves me well,
Satisfaction, has cast its spell.

Ashes from fiery bridges drift,
As stoic winds whisper and shift.
Desire and passion crash and burn.
New paths are laid from lessons learned.

I was born to seek and explore,
And expose every secret door.
I forge ahead and don't look back,
And hope no dark clouds haunt my tracks.

THE COURT ROOM

Viewers gather, interest rides high.
They seek the truth and reasons why.
They show concerned to hear the case,
About true love that's been erased.

A voice fills the room Loud and clear.
The time has come, the judge appears.
He enters with a Monarch air
He gracefully glides to his chair.

His gavel taps rhythmically
His voice reflects authority
His call for order; magic word
Unwanted noise is now unheard

As sides dig in and launch their fight
They both proclaim that they are right.
Spectators are awed and amazed,
Some unbelieving, some are dazed.

Witnesses add their components,
Facts unfolds moment to moment.
Lawyers proclaim they have the proof.
Witnesses swear to tell the truth.

Stakes are high, the drama rises
As each counselor surmises.
Guilty or not, what will it be?
The jury makes us wait to see.

FAMILY REUNION

Laughter filled the air with ringing elation
Found connections, showed thoughts and directions,

Strangers met and shared so much,
As DNA guided loves touch.
This family knew love at first sight,
And shared histories brought new light.

The time was right
The family was ready.
Conversations were light
And love ran steady.

Reconnecting to years gone past
To build new bonds we pray will last.
Collective intellect that grows
From family roots our talent flows.

Quickly bonding by the dozens
As we meet new unknown cousins.
In distant realities I see,
These souls who all connect to me.

Not one single bad attitude
Stopped the show or changed the mood.
New love and respect stole the show,
And showed us what we had to know.

We partners of shared DNA,
Got to bond in the family way.
That is how it should always be
When roots join at the family tree.

EPIPHANY

I just awoke in my bed
Normally, not something to dread.
But just how it all came to be
To me is still a mystery.

And I find myself quite distressed;
However, did I get undressed?
What really brings fear to my mind
Is unaccounted and lost time.

I remember speaking in slurs.
After that it became a blur.
My drinking became a project,
And the process took my logic.

Some men will do some insane things,
When drinks are poured and glasses cling.
For me no more whiskey and wine.
I promise this is my last time.

Real life is enough mystery,
Without losing reality.
Can't remember the time I lost,
Nor will I ever know the cost.

In spite of reckless behavior,
I must have had my own savior.
I think I finally realize,
That the drunkest drunk wins no prize.

WORRIED MIND

I worry about fools who break rules
And gun down little kids in school.
Their flawed and damage intellect
Commit to evil without regret.

Don't ask what their motives might be,
No reasons come with treachery.
Such cowards have insane logic,
When they make death their pet project.

I regret that politicians will
Assume the role of magicians,
And disappear when things get rough,
When they've taken more than enough.

They wear the mask of hypocrites,
And steal whatever they can get.
Furtive faces hide perversions.
Civil talk conceals diversions.

I worry about atheist,
And all the faith that they dismiss.
They see beliefs as sheer nonsense.
Their aimless spin voids their conscience.
Life is sad when values are lost
Dark drifting hearts will pay a cost.

I worry that there's no widespread love,
And most of us can't rise above
Those who could lend help just don't care.
They hoard fortunes and they won't share.
Their money they use to keep score,
They look with contempt at the poor.

I worry I might never find
That special one that's on my mind.
And If by chance she passed my way
Would I know the right words to say?

I worry about the planet
And the selfish men who run it,
And those dark souls who seek the light,
When they should remain out of sight.

Who speak of peace and harmony
Then boost war technology.
They ignore economic plight,
While war after war send men to fight.

Patriotism and loyalty
Are key words by which we rally,
But such words are footnotes that fade
Once we discern those debts they've made.

Leaders are lost and failure bound,
No sound Idea gets off the ground.
I worry that we've lost all trust.
And every heart has grown a crust.

I fret that some swollen egos
Will chart some course that no one knows,
To feel rapture without measure.
And on the heels of this pleasure.

I worry that we shall never find
Politicians with adult minds,
Who won't trade moral fiber.
For pieces of silver times forty.

America has lost the dream.
Selfish chaos is now the theme.
Lost is the quality of life.
Poverty cuts like a sharp knife.

I worry most of all that
Our great country is doomed to fall.
Even though we give it much praise
Are we Rome in our final days?
I really worry about things like that.

PEACE OF MIND

You can't teach it and they can't catch it.
You can't clone it and they can't match it.
It's something that we need to know
For ourselves and not just for show.

Real peace of mind you get to see
When petty worries turn and flee.
The warmth of constant sun like phase
Will raise the level of your days.

Your mind can feel it all so clear.
You delve in it and linger there.
Your settled spirit feels content.
Enjoying every moment spent.

You know how much it all means.
Heart and spirit feel light and clean.
With power like a wondrous kiss,
It touches you with constant bliss.

You wish some way you could share.
You wish you had extra to spare.
You know for sure that it is rare,
And so you handle it with care.

It becomes a strength inside you,
That tells your heart just what to do.
A sense of feeling nothing wrong,
This attitude will linger long.

But first you must know yourself,
And not be swayed by someone else.
Depending on decisions you make,
You'll know if you got what it takes.

Examples of Rhyme Scheme from Literature...

Rhyme Definition and uses.

There several definitions and uses to work with:
    1.Rhyme is a similar sound or the same sound in two or more words, most often in the final syllables or lines of a poem
    2.Rhyme is a repetition of similar sounding words occurring at the end of lines in poems
    3.Rhyme is a word tool that uses repetitive patterns to bring rhythm to musical lyrics and poems which differentiate them from prose.
    4. A rhyme is employed for the specific purpose of rendering a pleasing effect to a poem, which makes its recital an enjoyable experience.

The rhymes recognized by purists are "true rhymes":
1. masculine rhyme, in which the two words end with the same vowel–consonant combination (*stand / land*),

2. feminine rhyme (sometimes called double rhyme), in which two syllables rhyme (*profession / discretion*), and trisyllabic rhyme, in which three syllables rhyme (*patinate / latinate*).

The too-regular effect of masculine rhyme is sometimes softened by using trailing rhyme, or semirhyme, in which one of the two words trails an additional unstressed syllable behind it (*trail / failure*). *ure* would be the unstressed syllable

Other types of rhyme include

3.Eye Rhyme, in which syllables are identical in spelling but are pronounced differently (*cough / slough   good / food*)

4. Pararhyme, first used systematically by the 20th-century poet Wilfred Owen, in which two syllables have different vowel sounds but identical <u>penultimate</u> and final consonantal groupings (*grand / grind*).

5.Feminine pararhyme has two forms, one in which both vowel sounds differ, and one in which only one does (*ran in / run on*; *blindness / blandness*).

Weakened, or unaccented, rhyme occurs when the relevant syllable of the rhyming word is unstressed (*bend / frightened*). Because of the way in which lack of stress affects the sound, a rhyme of this kind may often be regarded as *alternate title rhyme*.

Serious efforts and imagination tend to present more colorful images with rhyming words. We as a society are enchanted with rhyming, which is like a musical chord on the ear of the listener. That's why it's no accident that most songs as well as most poems have rhyming words. Even gangster wrap rhymes.
Then there's that soothing flow of uniform balance that protrudes into the senses, which also makes poems easier to commit to memory. Songs and poems are memorized because of the rhyme scheme. Master piece poems come when logic is presented with rhyme schemes that capture the audience and motivates their thinking process.

Please note that it is important that you use a set rhyme scheme when you have the basis for a new poem. The execution of a rhyme scheme eliminates awkward rhymes that seemed tact on, and dangling along with ambiguous orphan ideas. With a solid and profound themes, a poem will almost write itself. In such cases the theme has to be wide range in order to feed the mind with layers of ideas to transform to verses. Remember to always stress the relevant syllable of the rhyming word in order to create a strong and well accented poem.

As poets and writers with imagination, we challenge ourselves to write better and to use rhymes effectively to express our ideas and not just for the sake of rhyming. As writers who tend to write rhyming poetry, we must take that extra step and make serious efforts. Rhyming is nice but so are ideas and new messages that stimulate and inspire.

Some people prefer non rhyming poems, and their style still promotes the art and their expressions are often filled with imagery. It's a great form of expression and I've tried to do non rhymes, but I am hopelessly addicted to searching for that right rhyme to go with the ideas that I hope will enrich each verse.. Remember to never feel frustrated if you can't master every phase of poetry. We should all be thankful for the gift that has been bestowed upon us all.

There are many reasons why you might choose to use rhyme:
To give pleasure. Rhyme, done well, is pleasing to the ear. It adds a musical element to the poem, and creates a feeling of "rightness," of pieces fitting together. It makes a poem easier to memorize, since the rhyme echoes in the reader's mind afterward, like a melody.

When the last word in a line of poetry rhymes with the last word in another line, this is called an <u>end rhyme</u>.

When words in the middle of a line of poetry rhyme with each other, this is called an <u>internal rhyme</u>.

True rhymes and off-rhymes
"Smart" and "art"; "fellow" and "yellow"; "surgery" and perjury" -- these are all examples of *true rhymes*, or *exact rhymes* because the final vowel and consonant sounds (or the final syllables in the longer words) are exact matches to the ear.

"Fate" and "saint"; "work" and "spark"; are examples of *off-rhymes*, or *slant-rhymes*. In each case, part of the sound matches exactly, but part of it doesn't. Off-rhymes use *assonance* and *consonance*:

    Assonance is a similarity between vowel sounds (the sounds made by your breath, written with the letters a,e,i,o,u,and sometimes y) "Sing, "lean", and "beet" are an example of assonance because they all have a similar "e" sound. Another example is "boat,"bone", and "mole," which all have a similiar "o" sound.

Consonance is a similarity between consonant sounds (consonants are the letters that you pronounce with your lips or tongue, not with your breath: b,c,d,f,g,h,j,k,l,m,n,p,q,r,s,t,v,w,x,z and sometimes y). "Lake,"book", and "back" are an example of consonance because even though the vowel sounds in these words are different, they all have the same "K" sounds.

When the same consonants are used at the beginning of the word (for example, the words "sing" and "sell"), that is called *alliteration*. consonance, which occurs when the two words are similar only in having identical final consonants (*best / least*).

You might choose to use off-rhymes instead of true rhymes, or in addition to them, to create a subtler effect. Using off-rhymes also gives you more choices of words to rhyme. This often makes it possible to create more original or surprising rhymes. How many pop songs can you think of that rhyme "heart" with "apart?" And when you hear the words "heaven above" in a song, you can bet that the word "love" is lurking nearby. There are only a few words that rhyme with "love," so they are used over and over again. Off-rhymes can help to remove some of that predictability so that you can come up with more interesting rhyme.

Have You Mastered all 7 of these Basic Rhyme Schemes?
Try a fresh new rhyme scheme.
Whether you're writing poetry, rap lyrics, or songs in any musical genre, different rhyme schemes draw different material out of you.
Trying out a new rhyme scheme forces you out of your usual writing habits and leads
to new discoveries. For both poets and songwriters, a new rhyme scheme also creates fresh patterns of suspense and release, just like a chord progression does. Rhyme can make words themselves sound beautifully musical — so you can write lyrics that almost sing themselves.

Below I've listed six basic four-line rhyme schemes for you to experiment with. Schemes you're unfamiliar with may feel a bit strange at first, but stick with them–they can lead to real breakthroughs in your poetry or song lyric writing.

Update: as of May 2015, I'm extending this post with more in-depth explanation of each scheme, along with classic examples and poetic forms that use each scheme. Progress as of today:, AABB, AAAA, AXAA, ABBA, AXXA.

ABAB

ABAB is a classic, often-used rhyme scheme with interlocking rhymes. It's sometimes called *alternate rhyme*.

To write in the ABAB rhyme scheme:
- Rhyme line 1 with line 3
- Rhyme line 2 with line 4

Here's an example of ABAB in action, as written by William Shakespeare:

A   O, if I say, you look upon this verse,
B   When I, perhaps, compounded am with clay,
A   Do not so much as my poor name rehearse,
B   But let your love even with my life decay...

This ABAB rhyme scheme is built into the famous poetic form called the Shakespearean sonnet.

XAXA

I've been down more than I've been up
This life ain't what you thought it was
We've lost touch with all charity
And people hurt you just because

This scheme's a little unpredictable, because it has *two* lines that don't rhyme with anything. This allows the writer (that's you!) a little more creative freedom. The two non-rhymed lines allow you to focus on what you really mean to say in your lyric.

To write in the XAXA rhyme scheme:
- Rhyme line 2 with line 4
- Make sure that lines 1 and 3 *don't* rhyme with each other or with any other line

XAXA is the rhyme scheme followed by
a traditional poetic form called the <u>ghazel.</u>
<u>AABB</u>

This scheme divides a section of four lines into two
rhymed couplets, each of which sounds kind of
complete in itself.
AAAA
I'm peaceful as a dove
Don't want to push and shove
I think I'm guilty of
A special kind of love
This one's tough to pull off. To relieve monotony,
you might try making some of the lines much shorter
than the others—varying line length will make it
sound less predictable.
AXAA, or AAXA
The world's gone to pot, no one cares
They hold what they got, no one shares
It seems that they will never learn
To treat brothers and sisters fair

One of the lines in each of these schemes is left
hanging. This scheme contains a bit of tension — try
it and see.
AAXA is found in the Persian poetic form called the
ruba'i.
ABBA
There's one thing that I know for sure,
It's special when a gorgeous girl,
Takes a chance and gives you a whirl,
That opens up a magic door.

A rhyming pair sandwiched inside of another
rhyming pair. This scheme's also known as *enclosed
rhyme*.

The AABA rhyme scheme is found in the poetic form called the Petrarchan sonnet.
AXXA
Love is the way of the world
Yet defies all description
In the midst of confusion
Grownup men will swoon and swirl.

Like XAXA above, AXXA allows the writer some extra creative freedom. The two middle lines are unpredictable; they don't rhyme with each other or any other line in the stanza.
This one's a personal favorite of mine; I like the way those two middle lines keep the audience in suspense until the last line finally releases the tension.
Exercise
If you've been mostly using ABAB and AABB like I did for years, try one of the rhyme schemes above for the verses of a new lyric. Write the scheme at the top of a blank page and get started. If you need a song idea, no worries—you can free write until an interesting lyric premise falls out.
Related Topics

Types of Rhyme Scheme

There are a number rhyme schemes used in poetry; however, some of the popular ones are:

- **Alternate rhyme:** It is also known as ABAB rhyme scheme, it rhymes as "ABAB CDCD EFEF GHGH."

- **Ballade:** It contains three stanzas with rhyme scheme of "ABABBCBC" followed by "BCBC."

- **Monorhyme:** It is a poem in which every line uses the same rhyme scheme.

- **Couplet:** It contains two line stanzas with "A, A," rhyme scheme that often appears as "A,A, B,B, C,C and D,D…"

- **Triplet:** It often repeats like a couplet, uses rhyme scheme of "AAA."

- **Enclosed rhyme:** It uses rhyme scheme of "ABBA"

- **Terzarima rhyme scheme:** It uses tercets, three lines stanzas. Its interlocking pattern on end words follow: Aba bcb cdc ded and so on…

- **Keats Odes rhyme scheme:** In his famous odes, Keats used a specific rhyme scheme, which is "ABABCDECDE."

- **Limerick:** A poem uses five lines with rhyme scheme of "AABBA."

- **Villanelle**: A nineteen-line poem consisting of five tercets and a final quatrain is villanelle and uses rhyme scheme of "A1bA2, abA1, abA2, abA1, abA2, abA1A2."

colophon

Brought to you by Wider Perspectives Publishing, care of James Wilson, with the mission of advancing the poetry and creative community of Hampton Roads, Virginia.
See our production of works from ...

Tanya Cunningham
    (Scientific Eve)
Lisa Kendrick
Nich (Nicholis Williams)
Terra Leigh
Taz Waysweete'
Bobby K.
    (The Poor Man's Poet)
J. Scott Wilson (TEECH!)
Charles Wilson

Jorge Mendez & JT Williams
Sarah Eileen Williams
Stephanie Diana (Noftz)
the Hampton Roads
    Artistic Collective
Jason Brown (Drk Mtr)
Martina Champion
Tony Broadway
Edith Blake
Crickyt J. Expression

    ... and others to come soon.

We promote and support the artists of the 757
  from the seats, from the stands,
  from the snapping fingers and clapping hands
  from the pages, and the stages
  and now we pass them forth to the ages

Check for the above artists on FaceBook, the Virginia Poetry Online channel on YouTube, and other social media.
Hampton Roads Artistic Collective is the non-profit extension of WPP and strives to simultaneously support worthy causes in Hampton Roads and the creative artists

www.ingramcontent.com/pod-product-compliance
Lightning Source LLC
Chambersburg PA
CBHW020941090426
42736CB00010B/1221